## Poems From
## The West Midlands
Edited by Angela Fairbrace

First published in Great Britain in 2007 by:
Young Writers
Remus House
Coltsfoot Drive
Peterborough
PE2 9JX
Telephone: 01733 890066
Website: www.youngwriters.co.uk

All Rights Reserved

© Copyright Contributors 2007

SB ISBN 978-1 84431 104 0

# Foreword

Young Writers was established in 1991 and has been passionately devoted to the promotion of reading and writing in children and young adults ever since. The quest continues today. Young Writers remains as committed to the nurturing of poetic and literary talent as ever.

This year's Young Writers competition has proven as vibrant and dynamic as ever and we are delighted to present a showcase of the best poetry from across the UK and in some cases overseas. Each poem has been selected from a wealth of *Little Laureates* entries before ultimately being published in this, our sixteenth primary school poetry series.

Once again, we have been supremely impressed by the overall quality of the entries we have received. The imagination, energy and creativity which has gone into each young writer's entry made choosing the poems a challenging and often difficult but ultimately hugely rewarding task - the general high standard of the work submitted ensured this opportunity to bring their poetry to a larger appreciative audience.

We sincerely hope you are pleased with this final collection and that you will enjoy *Little Laureates Poems From The West Midlands* for many years to come.

# Contents

**Highclare St Paul's School, Sutton Coldfield**
| | |
|---|---|
| Edward Bowen  (10) | 1 |
| Saumitra Awasthi  (10) | 2 |
| Avishay Mehra  (10) | 3 |
| Oliver Hobin  (10) | 4 |
| Peter Davie  (9) | 5 |
| William Carless  (10) | 6 |
| Kristian Quirke  (9) | 7 |
| Sam Burke  (9) | 8 |
| James Lesshafft  (10) | 9 |
| Kristian Scott  (11) | 10 |
| Suhayb Hussain  (10) | 11 |
| Daniel Offen  (11) | 12 |
| Kyran Kanda  (11) | 13 |
| Akshay Jain  (10) | 14 |

**Ravensdale Primary School, Coventry**
| | |
|---|---|
| Jordan Blacow  (10) | 15 |
| Avani Sohal  (10) | 16 |
| Elizabeth Rammell  (10) | 17 |
| James Smith  (10) | 18 |
| Zach Maguire  (10) | 19 |
| Jyoti Sumal  (10) | 20 |
| Thomas Killestein  (10) | 21 |
| Sophie Swords  (9) | 22 |
| Melissa Boulton  (9) | 23 |
| Ellen Davison  (9) | 24 |
| Sarah Cribdon  (10) | 25 |
| Alex Wright  (9) | 26 |
| Jakob Hegeland  (9) | 27 |
| Faisal Ahmed  (10) | 28 |
| Hannah Hoffman  (9) | 29 |
| Amy Hunter  (9) | 30 |
| Harry McAlister  (10) | 31 |
| Satveer Bhella  (10) | 32 |
| Aidan Mailer  (9) | 33 |
| Maria Frazer  (10) | 34 |
| Molly Deegan  (10) | 35 |
| Jake Hoare  (11) | 36 |

| | |
|---|---|
| Lauren Moore  (11) | 37 |
| Lora James  (11) | 38 |
| Matthew Harris  (10) | 39 |
| Kavita Patel  (10) | 40 |
| Kerrie Rosser  (11) | 41 |
| Megan Sizer  (10) | 42 |
| Steven Crosby  (10) | 43 |
| Dominic Hadley  (10) | 44 |
| Naomi Headley  (10) | 45 |
| Robyn Turner  (10) | 46 |
| Luke Wishart  (10) | 47 |
| Adam Smith  (9) | 48 |
| Liam McGhie  (9) | 49 |
| Corinne Gaggini  (11) | 50 |
| Thomas Cutler  (10) | 51 |
| Amrah Iqbal  (9) | 52 |
| Sophie Stone  (10) | 53 |

**SS John & Monica Primary School, Moseley**

| | |
|---|---|
| Khari Campbell-Lawrence  (9) | 54 |
| Amika Barnett  (8) | 55 |
| Priya Kaur Digpal  (9) | 56 |
| Shabinz Hirji  (9) | 57 |
| Catherine Egan  (10) | 58 |
| Chloe McNeil  (10) | 59 |
| Fatema Zahraz Shivji  (10) | 60 |
| Ayor Atoc-Adol  (9) | 61 |
| Michael Brown  (10) | 62 |
| Ishaq-Ul Rob  (7) | 63 |
| Syan Sue Bateman  (8) | 64 |
| Puja Kaur Digpal  (10) | 65 |
| Gabrielle Thomas  (11) | 66 |
| Hashim Malik  (10) | 67 |
| Kiarna Hendrickson  (10) | 68 |
| Katie Booth  (10) | 69 |
| Khuram Ali  (10) | 70 |
| Hakeem Ebrahim  (11) | 71 |
| Shiane Corbett  (10) | 72 |
| Georgia-Mae Coffey  (10) | 73 |
| Qudsiya Gulbarge  (11) | 74 |
| Jourdon Copeland  (10) | 75 |

| | |
|---|---|
| Libby Whittingham (10) | 76 |
| Jazmin Copeland (10) | 77 |
| Sophie Stevens (10) | 78 |

**St John's CE Primary School, Dudley**

| | |
|---|---|
| Katie Ludlam (9) | 79 |
| Rebecca McHale (10) | 80 |
| Megan Pritchard (11) | 81 |
| Georgie Roper (11) | 82 |
| Georgina Kovacs (10) | 83 |
| Priyesh Patel (11) | 84 |
| Sophie Williams (11) | 85 |
| Michael Sayers (11) | 86 |
| Rachel Campion (11) | 87 |
| Pippa Humphrey (10) | 88 |
| Georgette Rudge (10) | 89 |
| Alexandra Robinson (9) | 90 |
| Mitchell McCarthy (9) | 91 |
| Steph Robertson (8) | 92 |
| Abigail Fear (10) | 93 |
| Matthew Sayers (8) | 94 |
| Luke Stanford (9) | 95 |
| Georgie Evans (8) | 96 |

**Tividale Community Primary School, Tividale**

| | |
|---|---|
| Mutsa Ashley Nyamhunga (7) | 97 |
| Nicole Majcherczyk (7) | 98 |
| Zak Tyler (7) | 99 |
| Gurvinder Singh (8) | 100 |
| Ekam Sandhu (8) | 101 |
| Courtney Bowen (7) | 102 |
| Hansjit Heer (8) | 103 |
| Pavandeep Uppal (9) & Helaina Padda (10) | 104 |
| Smea Khan (10) | 105 |
| Priya Shrivastav (10) | 106 |
| Demi Marriner (9) | 107 |
| Emma Stephenson (10) | 108 |
| Jhanee Wilkins (10) | 109 |
| Simrun Bains (10) | 110 |
| Luqman Ahmed (7) | 111 |
| Satnam Kaur (9) | 112 |

| | |
|---|---|
| Idris Hussain  (9) | 113 |
| Olivia Sodhi  (10) | 114 |
| Christopher Lal  (10) | 115 |
| Nick Evans  (10) | 116 |
| Nathan Biran  (10) | 117 |
| Dhiren Patel  (9) | 118 |
| Rebecca Shepherd  (9) | 119 |
| Kiranpreet Hayer  (10) | 120 |
| Hussnain Anwar  (10) | 121 |
| Abbey Glancey  (9) | 122 |
| Ben Millward  (10) | 123 |
| Kieran Bowen  (9) | 124 |
| Jaspreet Kaur Rayat  (7) | 125 |
| Gurpreet Kaur  (7) | 126 |
| Jordan Basra | 127 |
| Samvir Sandhu  (9) | 128 |
| Prabhjeet Gill  (8) | 129 |
| Sharonjit Kaur Dhinsa  (8) | 130 |
| Zaina Yousaf  (8) | 131 |
| Parvathan Singh Biran  (7) | 132 |
| Navina Sahota  (8) | 133 |
| Rajdeep Kaur Sahota  (8) | 134 |
| Nikki Grewal  (7) | 135 |
| Jaghuir Singh  (7) | 136 |
| Parris Rowley  (7) | 137 |
| Jamie Fulwell  (7) | 138 |
| Gian Randhawa  (8) | 139 |
| Katie Maria Ubhi  (7) | 140 |
| Kiran Sandhu  (10) | 141 |
| Kiranjit Kaur Rai  (9) | 142 |
| Priya Rai  (10) | 143 |
| Olivia Hall  (10) | 144 |
| Sanna Mahmood  (9) | 145 |
| Takudzwa Mudere  (10) | 146 |
| Natasha Thompson  (8) | 147 |
| Jerome Sylvester  (8) | 148 |
| Callum Welborn  (8) | 149 |
| Ranjna Dewit  (8) | 150 |
| Makaita Kanyuchi  (10) | 151 |
| Macauley Scott  (9) | 152 |
| Sukhjit Johal  (9) | 153 |
| Nuna Vondee Gohoho  (10) | 154 |

| | |
|---|---|
| Ishmael Huxtable-Rowe  (10) | 155 |
| Navdeep Kaur Heer  (10) | 156 |
| Niall Hughes  (9) | 157 |
| Laura Cowley  (9) | 158 |
| Bhavin Patel  (10) | 159 |
| Sonia Virk  (8) | 160 |

**Woodgate Primary School, Birmingham**

| | |
|---|---|
| Bethany Jones  (11) | 161 |
| Jamie Ashmore  (11) | 162 |
| Rosie Jones  (11) | 163 |
| Charlotte Whatmore  (10) | 164 |
| Daniel Hancock  (10) | 165 |
| Amy Le  (10) | 166 |
| Courtney Ward  (8) & Kodey Williams  (10) | 167 |
| Christopher Reeves  (11) | 168 |
| Gary Howard  (10) | 169 |
| Joshua Saunders  (10) | 170 |
| Calam Oakley  (11) | 171 |
| Amie Atkinson  (10) | 172 |
| Brendan Snow  (11) | 173 |
| Sophie Kelly  (10) | 174 |
| Nicole Goff  (11) | 175 |
| Christopher Fisher  (11) | 176 |
| Dylan Lee  (11) | 177 |
| Jack Bissell  (11) | 178 |
| Rebecca Allcott  (10) | 179 |
| Matthew Morgan  (11) | 180 |
| Jade Johnson  (10) | 181 |
| Lauren-Annie Lintott  (11) | 182 |
| Amy Harrison  (10) | 183 |
| Katie Donnelly  (10) | 184 |
| Natalie Eddington  (11) | 185 |
| Victoria Boucher  (11) | 186 |
| Jack Strutt  (11) | 187 |
| Jessica Cammack  (10) | 188 |
| Jennifer Hunt  (10) | 189 |

## The Poems

## The Disaster

I woke up one nice and sunny morning
Just as an autumnal day was dawning
I dressed in a hurry to go and play
And I pushed my brother out of the way
He suddenly went completely bonkers
He went mad and pelted me with conkers
Sadly though one hit me right in the eye
I fell to the ground, looking at the sky
I lay there in a painful bleary state
Completely unable to communicate
I was rushed off to this hospital guy
And hoped and prayed that he could save my eye
I was pushed in a cool room you stayed in
It reminded me of a lovely inn
It had a PS2 and TV too
It was completely too good to be true
After I got to know the very nice room
The other one was like a scary tomb
This is where the operation would start
My heartbeat went completely off the chart
The operation went extremely well
So I was no longer ill or unwell.

**Edward Bowen (10)**
Highclare St Paul's School, Sutton Coldfield

## The Disaster

One morning I woke up from my long sleep,
I stretched out my leg and jumped out of bed.
I observed the sky, so happy was I,
One bird sat chirping alone on our roof.
I ran down the stairs and I heard a noise,
I tried to listen where the sound came from.
*Oh no!* I thought, *someone must have got hurt,*
I took no notice and went to my school,
I arrived at school at nine o'clock sharp,
The light bulb burned and the walls were shining.
I retrieved my bag and went to my room,
We finished our work and looked in our bags.
The teacher told me to get out my work,
Suddenly I realised I had forgot!
I tried to explain this to my teacher,
'Oh Mrs Boster, I'm very sorry,
Please don't punish me, I've apologised.'
With that I pleaded as much as I could,
You're in detention!' the teacher shouted,
'There is nothing you can do about it.'
I tried bribing her as much as I could,
Unfortunately she did not listen.
She just gave me a one-hour detention,
This disaster is how it all ended.

**Saumitra Awasthi (10)**
**Highclare St Paul's School, Sutton Coldfield**

## The Disaster

Today was the day to visit the farm,
A place which is rather peaceful and calm.
When we left the school to get on the coach,
Kevin asked if he could be my partner.
We talked about a new show on TV,
Which both of us found very interesting.
When we had approached the stop at the farm,
I got out my sun hat and put it on.
The teacher told us that we could split up,
So I went right up to observe the pups.
They belonged to a black and white sheepdog,
Who was having a little snooze right now.
I heard the cows across the grassy path,
So I went and enjoyed myself a lot.
While I was admiring the brown calf,
The big cow came and did something on my shoe.
I went to fetch Kevin from the art room,
So we could go and see the maned horses.
Having seen the rabbits and the ducklings,
We had to go to the café for lunch.
While we were eating everyone was stunned,
For the smell had affected everyone.
As the class were searching, Edward had found
On my shoe, something that looked like wet mud.
The whole class and I went right up to it
And the stench travelled up our noses.
Now I had realised that it was cow dung
And it was time to wash my filthy shoe.
So as we walked all the way to the coach,
I scraped my filthy shoe across the ground.
When we had returned from the farm to school,
I was no more declared the greatest fool.

**Avishay Mehra (10)**
Highclare St Paul's School, Sutton Coldfield

## The Magic Box
*(Based on 'Magic Box' by Kit Wright)*

I will put in my box . . .
The slimy slug's slick trail,
The hard shiny shell of a snail,
The slimy centre of an oyster.

My box is made from bronze, silver and gold
With secrets in the corners.
The hinges are made from old pirates' ropes,
The lock is made from ice, the key is made from water.

I will put in my box . . .
The smell of the ocean,
The taste of the finest water,
The feel of the finest silk.

I will put in my box . . .
The sound of Bill Shankley's voice,
The first word of a child,
The goal of John Arne Risse.

**Oliver Hobin (10)**
**Highclare St Paul's School, Sutton Coldfield**

## The Disaster

In my home there was a brown Buddha mouse
But as far as the owner was concerned
She wished he was eaten by a cat
Small brown mouse decided to fight back
So the next day he ate her chocolates
It was the final straw, she blew her top
She got a pistol and shot him apart
But she did not know there was more than one
His friend called up a Buddha mice army
He trained his army to eat human flesh
They asked the god for all the blessings
But they did forget that she had four cats
They fled into their holes for TLC
There was tons of innocent blood spilt
One went back in time and told the mice
He could summon up fire at his fists
He taught the army to do magic spells
They turned the cats into flying piggies
They shot fire at them and ate them for tea
They bought some ketchup to go with the pig
That was the best pig I've tasted in years.

**Peter Davie (9)**
Highclare St Paul's School, Sutton Coldfield

## Daffodils

In my garden it isn't just the odd daffodil here and there,
It's masses of daffodils everywhere,
In the fields, by the pond,
In the woodland far beyond.
I want to know how many there are,
That cover the fields ever so far.
Maybe one hundred,
Maybe a million,
Maybe even a hundred billion.

**William Carless (10)**
Highclare St Paul's School, Sutton Coldfield

## The Magic Box
*(Based on 'Magic Box' by Kit Wright)*

I will put in my box . . .
The scary slithering smooth skin of a snake
The touch of an elephant's tusk
And the finest part of a rainbow.

I will put in my box . . .
A sparkling, smooth, shiny pot of gold
A FIFA football with shiny stars on it
And the smile of a baby.

I will put in my box . . .
A turtle with wings on its back
A spark of electric off an electric eel
And a slimy slithering squid.

I will put in the box . . .
A shark with a shell on its back
A grape off a grape vine
Snow off a snowy snowman's belly.

I will put in my box . . .
Juicy jelly wobbling on a plate
Sand of the Sahara Desert.

**Kristian Quirke (9)**
**Highclare St Paul's School, Sutton Coldfield**

# The Magic Box
*(Based on 'Magic Box' by Kit Wright)*

I will put in my box . . .
A new box season special and better than the others
The great London Eye
And fast electric to give me a shock.

I will put in my box . . .
The great giant world
A giant orange tree
A giant white puddle to get wet.

I will put in my box . . .
A very small fountain
And a big mountain
And a huge planet.

I will put in my box . . .
A big chubby alien
And a green sun
And a yellow moon.

I will put in my box . . .
A sixth sense super and superior to the others
A new emotion
And new soap with an old house.

**Sam Burke (9)**
**Highclare St Paul's School, Sutton Coldfield**

## James

There was a boy called James
Who wasn't very tame
And once he went on stage
Then fainted as he gazed
*Thump!* James had fallen off stage
It's a catastrophe
The crowd was really shocked
As soon as that happened
The whole room was empty
All the others were mad
James had wrecked the whole play
Everyone was shouting
'Stop!' he shouted loudly
Then he ran off back home
He wept and wept till dawn
Then when the sun rose up
Water was all over
Water was flooding streets
James was so upset now
Please pull it together
James tried and tried to stop
And finally he stopped
The people were filled with joy
There were celebrations
Form Hong Kong to London.

**James Lesshafft (10)**
**Highclare St Paul's School, Sutton Coldfield**

# Daydreams

Mrs Beck thinks I'm watching,
Oh no, I'm soaring off a turnbuckle onto the Undertaker's stomach.
I'm attacking a huge mummy trying to take over the world.
I'm darting through the Grand Prix final.
I'm diving off a cruise ship into the shadowy depths of the ocean.

Mr Robinson thinks I'm listening,
But I'm swimming in a melted chocolate ocean.
I've just fired in a 30-yarder in the World Cup final.
I'm flying to America in a jumbo jet.
I'm propelling myself off a cliff into the sea in search of treasure.

Mrs Beck thinks I'm paying attention,
I'm actually on top of a big blue whale.
I'm springing myself into a five-metre deep pool of cash.
KO! I've just knocked out the champion boxer himself.
I'm tightrope walking on a twenty-metre high rope.
Uh oh! I've just knocked my desk over, I'm in for it now!

**Kristian Scott (11)**
**Highclare St Paul's School, Sutton Coldfield**

# Daydreams

Mrs Beck thinks I'm writing poetry
but I'm fighting aliens on Mars
I'm diving in the Atlantic Ocean
getting chased by sharks . . .
I'm fishing for trout
I've caught ten
and going home late . . .
Being the boxing champion.

Mr Robinson thinks I'm doing VR
but no
I'm throwing blueberry pies at circus performers
I'm wrestling a tiger
racing a cheetah
I'm jumping out of a plane.

I think of racing my friends on quad bikes . . .
I'm the Prime Minister of the UK
I'm racing the police
and I crash into a tree
When I wake up
I find I've been hit by a rubber.

**Suhayb Hussain (10)**
**Highclare St Paul's School, Sutton Coldfield**

# Daydreams

Mrs Beck thinks I'm reading
but I'm wresting crocodiles
or racing cheetahs . . .
I'm floating in a spacecraft
or parachuting from a plane.
I'm finding a rare dinosaur fossil
or jumping like a kangaroo.
I'm pursuing a monster from the deep
who is cascading through the water.

Mrs Beck thinks I'm writing -
but no
I'm lifting the FA Cup
or I'm racing Michael Schumacher.
I'm running for my life.
I'm getting homework
or I'm a ghost, scaring everyone
or going to a premiere.
I am a wizard charming all girls to like me.

I'm Isaac Newton discovering gravity
or I'm in a distant land saving my love.
My love is screaming
but wait
it's Mrs Beck shouting at me.

**Daniel Offen (11)**
**Highclare St Paul's School, Sutton Coldfield**

# Daydreams

Mr Robinson thinks I'm doing VR
but I'm not.
I'm directing a five-star production . . .
performing at the Old Rep.
Writing a book which sells like lightning.
Fighting in the RAW heavyweight finals
winning - now I've got the belt in my hand
people screaming for me.

Mr Robinson thinks I'm doing corrections
but I'm not.
I'm fighting a shark for my life.
Living in the Stone Age.
Saving a train with a bomb on it.
Signing autographs because I'm a famous author.
I'm completing a mission because I'm a spy.

Mrs Beck thinks I'm doing a maths exam
I'm not.
I'm fighting Count Dracula.
I'm eating sugary doughnuts.
I'm saving a baby from drowning.
I'm . . . 'Kyran!'
Oh no, I've just soaked Mr Robinson, *sorry!*

**Kyran Kanda (11)**
**Highclare St Paul's School, Sutton Coldfield**

# Daydreaming

Mrs Beck thinks I'm writing poetry
but I'm flying in the air
or swimming in a deep, dark ocean
I'm having a chase with a shark
and a gigantic killer whale . . .
I wash up on the shore
with a million cuts and bites all over my body.

Mr Robinson thinks I'm doing VR
but I'm having a mud fight with my brother . . .
or sky-diving from a jet plane
I'm shooting like a rocket in the air
I'm landing with a crash
forgetting to pull up my parachute
I've just sprained my ankle
but I give the audience a thumbs up
to show them that I'm OK.

I think of driving a Ferrari
the wind making my lips flap about
500mph, way over the speed limit
or I'm the world's superhero
saving the Earth from mass destruction
When I stir
the teacher's shouting -
I'm feeling embarrassed.

**Akshay Jain (10)**
**Highclare St Paul's School, Sutton Coldfield**

## Silence

Silence sounds like a wave crashing into the shore.
Silence feels like a breath of fresh air running up your face.
Silence tastes like fresh air in an open field.
Silence looks like an empty box.
Silence reminds me of a deserted house.

**Jordan Blacow (10)**
**Ravensdale Primary School, Coventry**

# Laughter

The sound of laughter is like the sound of happiness, giggles and funny jokes all around.
Laughter feels like a strange feeling approaching the inside of your body and shares a lovely feeling.
Laughter tastes like a delicious mint choc chip ice cream melting in a child's mouth on a scorching hot day.
It smells like the petrol from the engine of the ice cream van entering your nose.
Laughter reminds me of the good times that happened when I was a little girl and with my friends and family.

**Avani Sohal (10)**
**Ravensdale Primary School, Coventry**

## Fun

Fun is like the smell of children
playing and laughing in the park.

Fun tastes like yummy sweets
from the corner shop.

Fun looks like a happy fairy tale,
like the story of Snow White.

Fun reminds us of love and laughter.
Fun sounds like a tuneful flute
playing in a sweet choir.

**Elizabeth Rammell (10)**
Ravensdale Primary School, Coventry

# Silence . . .

Silence is nothing,
you might hear it one day,
Silence is like thin air.
Silence sounds like nothing,
it is absolutely bare.

Silence is like feeling emptiness,
it naturally surrounds you
if you are as quiet as an ant.

Silence is the image of darkness,
it is souls dancing and singing,
they are so loud yet so quiet,
'tis silence, yes silence 'tis.

Silence tastes like anything
like water it takes the shape of where it is,
it will go with you all of the time,
just be silent and it will be there.

Silence reminds you of your previous life,
your moments you have enjoyed,
just be silent, yes silent,
and they will come to you, yes them all.

**James Smith (10)**
**Ravensdale Primary School, Coventry**

## Fun!

Fun sounds like children having the time of their lives
Fun tastes like children eating sweets from the corner shop
Fun smells like children playing in the park
Fun looks like people having a great day
Fun feels like a happy fairy tale
Fun reminds me of my first kiss.

**Zach Maguire (10)**
**Ravensdale Primary School, Coventry**

# Silence

It was so quiet I could hear an army of ants marching
through a field of green grass.

It was so peaceful I could hear the silent letters in words
that reminds me of someone giving the silent treatment.

It was so dull I could hear creepy-crawlies running around
the garden which would taste very unpleasant.

It was so muted I could hear fresh bread out of the oven being sliced
which smells like nothing I have ever smelt before.

It was so lonely I could hear sweet wrappers being unwrapped
which feels like smooth and soft toffee.

**Jyoti Sumal (10)**
**Ravensdale Primary School, Coventry**

## Funny Fun Poem

Fun is like the sound of laughter, fairgrounds and ice cream trucks,
Whatever you say it's not for ducks.

Fun tastes like raspberry jam,
It doesn't taste a thing like lamb.

Fun smells like perfume,
Nothing like inevitable doom.

Fun looks like a group of balloons,
Unlike a group of sand dunes.

**Thomas Killestein (10)**
**Ravensdale Primary School, Coventry**

## Darkness

Darkness sounds like silence.
Darkness tastes like nothing but dirt.
Darkness smells like a bomb just landing on a poor innocent house
                                                         with people in.
It looks like nothing but dullness.
It feels like you have just been shot and you can't feel anything
                                                         but pain.

**Sophie Swords (9)**
**Ravensdale Primary School, Coventry**

## Sadness

Drowned in sad thoughts,
Gasping for breath,
The sound of silence
Is my beautiful thoughts' death.

I'm longing for life,
A thing so long and powerful,
Life isn't just living,
It's a long-lasting fable.

The long-lasting fable
Has been ended and sealed,
Rejected and forgotten,
Love is like a shield.

My shield is gone,
I'm easily hurt,
I am the head of all pessimists.

**Melissa Boulton (9)**
**Ravensdale Primary School, Coventry**

## Darkness

Darkness is black like a scary black hole,
Darkness is bitter like cold bitter air,
Darkness is smelly like dustbins wheeling to the dust cart,
Darkness is loud and scary like your worst nightmare,
Darkness is ugly like a scary witch's face,
Darkness is rough, tough skin wearing out,
Darkness reminds me of a scary black face creeping towards me.

**Ellen Davison (9)**
**Ravensdale Primary School, Coventry**

## Silence Of Silence

As the silence of silence
Is drawn over the sky
The long conversation stops
As the visitors say bye.

        As the silence of silence
        Is drawn over the ground
        When the pirates are stunned
        By the golden treasure they've found.

As the silence of silence
Is drawn over the table
When in the hospital stands
As a heart gives out like in a deadly fable.

**Sarah Cribdon (10)**
Ravensdale Primary School, Coventry

# Fear

It feels like a plane about to crash into a rock,
It tastes like the Great Fire of London is stuck in my mouth,
It sounds like a siren going through my ears and back 100 times,
It looks like a skull and crossbones glued onto my eyes
It smells like I'm trapped inside a coalmine.
*I have so much fear!*

**Alex Wright (9)**
**Ravensdale Primary School, Coventry**

## Darkness

The darkness looks black
Tastes of the plants in moving circles
The darkness reminds your mind of a dream
The darkness feels invisible
The darkness sounds breezy
The darkness is black and like a mountain.

**Jakob Hegeland (9)**
**Ravensdale Primary School, Coventry**

## Darkness Fades

I can feel the darkness fade
Like a sharp fearless blade
I can hear the sneaky wolf howl
Like a big wise owl.

I can smell the fear of myself
Like a little baby left with a spider
A big aeroplane flying in the darkness
Like a sharp glider.

I can taste the cold air
Rising on my tongue
I can feel the darkness fade
Like a big piece of fungi.

I can smell and feel the rising sun
Burning on my chest
As my body rises
The darkness has faded away.

**Faisal Ahmed (10)**
Ravensdale Primary School, Coventry

## Anger

Anger feels like a volcano erupting in your body
Anger sounds like an atom bomb dropping
Anger smells like a fire burning and killing innocent people
Anger looks like someone being killed
Anger reminds me of losing my family.

**Hannah Hoffman (9)**
**Ravensdale Primary School, Coventry**

## Anger

Anger sounds like a baby screaming angry for attention
Anger tastes like hot sauce burning a little girl's mouth
Anger smells like lava bubbling from a volcano
Anger looks like a fiery furnace melting iron to liquid
Anger feels like burning fire burning paper to ashes.

**Amy Hunter (9)**
**Ravensdale Primary School, Coventry**

# Laughter

Laughter sounds like a hyena having the time of its life
Laughter tastes like unstoppable fun
Laughter smells like a star in the beautiful midnight sky
Laughter looks like the biggest smile in the world
Laughter feels like my body is nothing without it
Laughter reminds me of millions of jokes laughing at once.

**Harry McAlister (10)**
**Ravensdale Primary School, Coventry**

## Anger

It sounds like a growling bear
It tastes like a lonely mayor
It smells like something burning
It looks like darkness appearing
It feels like anger is coming
It reminds me of someone dying.

**Satveer Bhella (10)**
Ravensdale Primary School, Coventry

## Anger

Red is the colour of anger,
It drives you up the wall.
It sounds like someone screaming down your ear with no care at all.
It smells like a pig getting burnt on a barbecue.
It reminds you of someone fighting for their life.
It tastes like someone's sweat dripping into your mouth.

**Aidan Mailer (9)**
**Ravensdale Primary School, Coventry**

## Silence

Silence sounds likes birds singing in the trees.
Silence smells like the salty seas.
Silence feels like a dress made of silk.
Silence tastes like soft caramel, ever so creamy.
Silence reminds me of a jungle with lots of wildlife, it's so dreamy.
Silence looks like a baby drinking milk.

**Maria Frazer (10)**
Ravensdale Primary School, Coventry

## My Monster

My monster is a football hog,
he's jumping all day like a frog.
I calm him down with Scooby Snacks,
but he still jumps around like a frog.
I'm proud of him, my tangerine,
why do I bother when he's just too full of beans?
At the end of the day he can be mean,
oh no, my secret monster's almost been seen.

**Molly Deegan (10)**
**Ravensdale Primary School, Coventry**

## Monster

M y house is full, 'Dinner, dinner,' it shall call
O h you must be careful you don't fall
N oge will hear his moanful call
S inister, huge, purple and hairy
T hundering through the house oh awfully scary
E at but be ever so wary
R ocky's greed is mean as mean.

**Jake Hoare (11)**
**Ravensdale Primary School, Coventry**

## Monsters In My House!

There's a routine that I follow
As I walk around my house,
I creep around on tiptoes
As quiet as a mouse.

The reason that I do this,
The reason I'm scared a lot
Is because there's monsters in my house,
They arrived with a flower pot.

There's a big ghoul in the attic,
There's a hairy thing downstairs,
There's a gigantic, slimy creature
That's obsessed with wooden chairs.

They creep around at daytime,
They haunt the kitchen by night,
When I'm in bed trying to sleep
They come to give me a fright.

**Lauren Moore (11)**
Ravensdale Primary School, Coventry

# My Monster

M y monster is as hairy as my uncle's back
O ld as a tree's branch
N asty as garbage
S melly as my grandad's shoe
T iny as a teaspoon
E very bit of her is as green as grass
R ude as a bat.

**Lora James (11)**
**Ravensdale Primary School, Coventry**

## My Monsters

I have a pet monster
Who eats my cat's food,
He keeps getting a tummy ache
So I feed him monster food.

I have a friend monster
Who likes monster chase,
But I always catch him
Because he has a slow pace.

I have a teacher monster
Who likes teaching us maths,
So I keep running
Down the school path.

I have a granny monster
Who acts all silly,
But I still don't understand
Why her name is Billy.

I have a dad monster
Whose behaviour is really bad,
He keeps on tripping up
So he feels really sad.

I have a neighbour monster
Who keeps on banging at my door,
So I keep thinking
That he might use a saw.

**Matthew Harris (10)**
Ravensdale Primary School, Coventry

## The Monster That Got Me Told Off

He lives in my drawer,
I don't know what to do,
He stays quiet
When I leave from school.

He shouts and rattles
The teacher thinks it's me,
He belches and trumps
And people laugh at me.

I got sent to the head teacher,
I got really scared,
Until I realised
There was no one there.

**Kavita Patel (10)**
**Ravensdale Primary School, Coventry**

## Monster Under My Bed

*Creak, creak* all night,
Under my bed, out of sight.
Green and yellow, ugly thing,
Wearing golden shiny bling.
Five feet tall, very smelly,
Just like my uncle's welly.
Eight antennas, eight eyes,
Always steals my mum's pies.
I tried to tell her at tea,
'It's my monster not me.'
'Don't be silly, don't lie,
You really did steal that pie.'
I heard that noise once more,
I turned around to face the door,
'Help me, help Fred!'
When I turned around my mum was dead.

**Kerrie Rosser (11)**
**Ravensdale Primary School, Coventry**

## The Night Monster

Rumbling like an earthquake,
Flickering street lamps,
Jumping out to scare the neighbours
And to stop the song and dance.

Bellowing as loud as a drum kit,
The monster would pounce and say,
'I'll eat you at sunrise,
Now don't go away.'

A blood-curdling scream,
A struggle to break free,
Who will live another night
And run away to the Isle of Wight?

**Megan Sizer (10)**
**Ravensdale Primary School, Coventry**

# Monsters

Monsters crazy
Monsters small
Monsters lazy
Monsters tall
Monsters scary
Monsters dumb
Monsters hairy
Monsters glum

But my monster seems to be
Someone who is just like me!

**Steven Crosby (10)**
**Ravensdale Primary School, Coventry**

## Monsters

Monsters scary
Monsters tall
Monsters hairy
Monsters small
Monsters crazy
Monsters fat
Monsters lazy
Monsters eat rats
But my monster is really my cat.

**Dominic Hadley (10)**
**Ravensdale Primary School, Coventry**

## The Lonely Monster

I am so lonely stuck up here,
But Mum says, 'Not to worry dear,
We'll move house - you just wait and see,'
It's just not easy being me.

I'm stuck up here all on my own,
(At least until my mum gets home.)
And then she rests in an easy chair,
Then softly strokes my long black hair.

I'm the ugliest kid in all the land,
If you were me you'd understand.
But my mum - she appreciates me,
It's just not easy being me.

**Naomi Headley (10)**
**Ravensdale Primary School, Coventry**

## Inside Me

Somewhere in here, inside of me,
I feel an urge to be let free.

I roam my labyrinth every day,
Then a voice in my head, seems to say.

'You won't be lonely or be bullied,
Just be yourself and don't be worried.

Now go out there and say it nicely,
You must not lie, just say it precisely!'

I ask them if we could be friends,
'No way,' they yell, 'please don't pretend.'

But what no one can realise
Is that it's dark down here - whilst lost inside.

I stroll home that night and lie on my bed,
Really stressed, I place my hands on my head.

At that moment I start to shiver,
So I get up and look in the mirror.

To my surprise, all I see,
Is someone normal, it is me!

**Robyn Turner (10)**
**Ravensdale Primary School, Coventry**

## Anger

Anger feels like a ferocious bear trapped inside you,
clawing and ripping itself out.
Anger sounds like a roaring lion defending its territory.
Anger tastes like burning ashes, scorching your mouth
as you try to speak.
Anger smells like a choking black smoke
which you can't escape from gassing up.
Anger looks like a monstrous tiger prowling its domain,
roaring at anyone who comes near.
Anger feels like fire ripping through you.
Anger reminds me of hatred and despair gouging in my head.

**Luke Wishart (10)**
**Ravensdale Primary School, Coventry**

## Anger's Happenings

Anger sounds like a mummy rising from the dead.
It tastes like a curry made from 100% spice.
Anger smells like mint ice cream with poison inside.
Anger looks like a tiger munching on its victim.
It feels like being abducted by aliens and never returning.
It reminds me of being crushed by a shelf and no one helping.

**Adam Smith (9)**
**Ravensdale Primary School, Coventry**

## Anger

Anger is frustration when you can't think what to write,
like you're trying and trying with all your might.
Anger looks like a bomb exploding,
a robber waiting for a safe decoding.
Anger smells like fire burning,
but nothing like some butter churning.
Anger tastes like an ice cream with dirt on,
unlike a very tasty bread scone.

**Liam McGhie (9)**
**Ravensdale Primary School, Coventry**

## My Monster!

M y monster is
O dourous
N otorious
S melly
T errifying
E normous
R abid

But I don't care
because the most important thing of all is
that he's my *monster!*

**Corinne Gaggini (11)**
Ravensdale Primary School, Coventry

## The Monster Poem

M ysterious
O dourous
N asty
S erious
T all
E nvious
R iotous

There's a monster that lives under my bed
He actually has a very big head,
Every night he comes out,
And then I run out the door, 'Mum!' I shout.

**Thomas Cutler (10)**
Ravensdale Primary School, Coventry

## Love And Life!

Fear is like a tear
Don't ever cry
A tear is very clear
Life is only cheery
There is a key to life like you and me can take
Love is like a dove
Sweet and nice as life itself
Water reminds me of the sea
But don't worry, relax with a cup of tea.

**Amrah Iqbal (9)**
**Ravensdale Primary School, Coventry**

## Love Is Strong As Death!

Love, a throbbing scarlet heart pierced by a silver arrow,
Jewelled eyes meet and dreamy thoughts flood minds,
Love is a taste of creamy rich chocolate filling your mouth,
The sleepy feeling of lying down on a bed of beautiful flowers.

Love is like an iced lily waving in the wind,
Smelling like the air is full of scented crimson roses,
A bluebird sings a sweet song as the sun is rising,
Will that great love end?

**Sophie Stone (10)**
**Ravensdale Primary School, Coventry**

# Wizard And Witch Poem

A witch as bald as a bat
Spilt her hair tonic over the mat
It's grown so much higher
She can't see the fire
And she thinks that it's smothered her cat.

There was an old wizard from Brazil,
Who always ate more than his fill,
He thought it no matter
That his waistline grew fatter,
But he burst, doesn't that make you ill?

**Khari Campbell-Lawrence (9)**
SS John & Monica Primary School, Moseley

## The Witch's Kitchen

Dirty and smelly,
When she cooks her cat goes wild,
She sits there mixing tonight's dinner,
All the rats suddenly appear,
She uses the bones of the children who live near,
They all run scared when they can hear,
The witch is laughing at their crying.

**Amika Barnett (8)**
SS John & Monica Primary School, Moseley

# Frogs

Frogs, frogs, almost like toads
My friend and I love them loads
Green and yellow, they are the best
We love them lots, they are better than the rest
I wish I could hold one
Morning and night
Mum would not like it
I know I'm right
Maybe one day my dream will come true
If not I'll always have the blues.

**Priya Kaur Digpal (9)**
SS John & Monica Primary School, Moseley

## Steamy Shower

I love a dreamy steamy shower
Hanging about for over an hour
Just before bed getting hot and red in the steam
Standing there with time to dream
Water running over me feeling drips dripping off the ceiling
Mum says it's my fault it's peeling
Nothing can beat the hot wet heat
Nothing wetter, nothing better
I love a dreamy steamy shower.

**Shabinz Hirji (9)**
**SS John & Monica Primary School, Moseley**

## The Scoron

Deep, deep down in the deep dark forest stands this castle.
Within it 'The Scoron', I won't describe it, you'll get a shock,
Your mind will freeze like a broken clock.
If you come across it at night
You're bound to get a big, big fright.
The silvery moon shines on its wings
And when it smells fire, it sings.
It's never as deadly as you think,
But be careful it can stink. Badly.
It lives in the grounds of the haunted castle,
Hint: Don't give it hassle.
*It's always ready to eat a human!*

**Catherine Egan (10)**
SS John & Monica Primary School, Moseley

## Dinner Time

Dinner time, dinner time,
My favourite time of the day.
Yummy in my tummy,
Just thinking of it makes me chubby,
Yummy in my tummy,
Fishfingers, burgers, soup, chips and pizza
Is just the creature.

**Chloe McNeil (10)**
**SS John & Monica Primary School, Moseley**

# Mother

M y mother is kind and sweet,
   to be with her is always a treat.

O ceans deep or mountains high, her love can never be measured,
   for she is a blessing that God has given us to treasure.

T oday is one of the days we get to tell her, 'Mum, to us you are truly dear,'
   was it not for her we would not be here.

H appy is how she wants us to be and live a good life,
   day and night for this she does strive.

E ven if one tried, there could be none like her for she is the best,
   whether tired or ill never taking a rest.

R emember today is a special day just for you mum
   and I hope with these few words I can tell you just how much
   you mean to me.

   I love you Mum, you mean the world to me,
   for you make the world a better place to be.

**Fatema Zahraz Shivji (10)**
SS John & Monica Primary School, Moseley

## Three Silly Things To Do With A Sock

Fill it with custard's lovely yellow stuff,
It will seep through the knitting
And gun up the fluff.

Wear it on your ear,
Let it wave and flap,
Or balance it on the top of your head
And say it is a cap.

Cook it for your tea,
Eat it with ketchup and with chips,
To show that you will enjoy it
Be sure to lick your lips.

**Ayor Atoc-Adol (9)**
SS John & Monica Primary School, Moseley

## School Is Horrible

School is horrible but I don't know why
So why don't you give it a try?
Why don't you go and see what you think?
It's got bright colours - blue, green, red and pink.
School's got science, literacy, maths and art
Sometimes it will tear you apart
When you go home I bet you'll be on the phone
Some children love school to bits but they hate bringing their PE kits
School is horrible to me so listen to me as you can see
*School is horrible!*

**Michael Brown (10)**
SS John & Monica Primary School, Moseley

## The Fluffy Brown Dog

A fluffy brown dog was chewing on my sock
It was all in pieces
When I heard a knock
Oh no, it's my dad, he will be very mad
Please run away, hide, be quick, disappear into the fog.

**Ishaq-Ul Rob (7)**
**SS John & Monica Primary School, Moseley**

# The Iron Man

The iron man was made of iron.
He had a head the shape of a dustbin but the size of a bedroom.
He had a body as big as a house.
He had eyes the size of dishwashers.
He had shoulders as big as hills.
He had arms as long as a ladder.
He had hands as big as tables.
He had buttons as big as men's heads.
He had legs as tall as skyscrapers.
He had feet as long and as wide as radiators.
That was the iron man.

**Syan Sue Bateman (8)**
SS John & Monica Primary School, Moseley

## Secondary School

I don't want to leave Year 6
Please Miss Cummings hide us quick
In the cupboards and behind the doors
In the trays and in the drawers.

Grown-ups say going to big school isn't scary
That's like saying gorillas aren't hairy
March the 1st is coming
That's the school that you're going to.

Leaving friends is hard
But adults say making new friends is a laugh
School's cool because of my friends
What am I going to do now? Is my life at an end?

I thought our uniforms were bad
But Swanhurst's uniform is really sad
The school I put down first I'm glad about
So that's my mixed feelings about secondary school.

**Puja Kaur Digpal (10)**
SS John & Monica Primary School, Moseley

## Snow - Haiku

It is really white
And it's really, really cold
So that's why it's snow.

**Gabrielle Thomas (11)**
SS John & Monica Primary School, Moseley

## Cats And Dogs

C lever at coming home
A lways outside on the fence
T heir tails are twisting every time
S ometimes sensible, sometimes not.

D ogs fight like two dragons
O utstanding from a far view
G oing for a walk with their families
S ensible sometimes.

**Hashim Malik (10)**
SS John & Monica Primary School, Moseley

## Don't Lie!

Don't lie because they will soon find out
When they do close your mouth
It's a bad thing to do
And comes back to you
When you're really, really sorry and you're about to cry
Calm down a bit and dry your eye
Remember that there's people out there that will forgive you
So remember this because we all love you!

**Kiarna Hendrickson (10)**
SS John & Monica Primary School, Moseley

## Secondary School

I never want to leave this school
that might sound mad but this school rules
Secondary school is big and scary
it's all crowded, but here it's airy
I never want to leave my friends
our friendship hopefully will never end
Please Lord let me stay
lock me up, hide me away
I will get the letter on March 1st
to find out where I will go, I hope it's not the worst.
Five days later I will be one year older
awaiting for my big blue folder.

**Katie Booth (10)**
**SS John & Monica Primary School, Moseley**

## My Acrostic About Teeth

T wisting and turning when you want to pull it out.
E ating and crunching hurts when you have a wobbly tooth.
E nd of the day when your tooth comes out the tooth fairy will come.
T o make your teeth shiny brush them.
H aving toothache makes you not eat anything.

**Khuram Ali (10)**
SS John & Monica Primary School, Moseley

## My Poem About Teeth

Teeth are very shiny,
You have to keep them clean,
Teeth are very white
And they're not green.
Teeth you have to keep clean
Or they're gonna rot,
Remember never cook them in a frying pot.
When you are tiny
Your teeth are very small,
They could come out
If they are hit by a ball.
When your teeth wobble
They could come out,
Tooth fairy ain't gonna come,
Probably too busy eating trout.

**Hakeem Ebrahim (11)**
**SS John & Monica Primary School, Moseley**

# Anticipation

What's it all about?
I mean the rhyming,
The description, the way every poet writes in a different way,
Why don't we just write poetry in the form of acrostics, haikus, personification?
What is poetry?
But then my voice and my heart rate slowly toned back down
to its normal level and my brain buzzed with anticipation
waiting for an answer to pop to the front of my head.
I closed my eyes hard and concentrated so hard
that I wouldn't know if I was in the mouth of a cannonball,
just to find out what a bunch of words meant.
And why people think it's so beautiful.
Then I open my eyes, my eyelashes twinkled
as the sun's ultraviolet rays slanted across my face.
I saw a man standing in a white cloak, looking into my eyes,
he said to me, 'Why do you spite the wonders of poetry?'
I answered back, 'Well, why do we have poetry?'
'We have it to describe all of the wonders on the Earth.
Look at the grass, it's as fluffy as a poodle, the apples on the trees
are as red as your cheeks,' he replied with a soft yet polite voice.
My head hung but my heart was filled with joy.

**Shiane Corbett (10)**
SS John & Monica Primary School, Moseley

## Her Coat

She throws her beauty all over the town,
While settling in the sky without a frown.
Her red coat and sunglasses too,
Her orange handbag is as big as you.
Her eyes are like flames
And Sun is her name.

She stays in the sky from dawn till dusk,
Then the moon will take her place, he is tough as a tusk.
He has striped blue pyjamas with a teddy bear too
And he sleeps in the sky while shining through.

I wake up in the morning knowing moon won't keep,
Moon will awake from his sleep.
Sun will come up from under the Earth,
She'll shine and shine for all she is worth.
This happens every day and every night,
Making me feel I'll be alright.

**Georgia-Mae Coffey (10)**
**SS John & Monica Primary School, Moseley**

# Weathers

Wherever you go there is a weather which everyone likes.
Early in the mornings you see the bright morning sun
and hear the birds singing along.
After it might rain as if the clouds are crying with great sorrow.
Tomorrow it might be that the buds might burst out like fireworks
with bright colours of spring.
Happily everyone rejoices until thunder comes along.
Enraged with horror as it sees what is going on in the world below.
Raindrops on the ground really loud like pennies and pounds.
Still it carries on through the night until the weather cycle
starts again.

**Qudsiya Gulbarge (11)**
SS John & Monica Primary School, Moseley

## School

S chool work always
C aring teachers
H omework all the time
O pen windows, people ask
O utside having fun with each other
L earning and having fun with your friends,
that's what school's about.

**Jourdon Copeland (10)**
SS John & Monica Primary School, Moseley

## SS John And Monica

S t John and Monica are our school saints, our
S chool is special in every way.

J oyful, sorrowful and happy memories are here from
when we started at this fantastic school.
O ur friends we met when we first started school
feel like family now.
H ow hard it is for some to picture themselves with no friends
and now a big bunch of them.
N ow stop and think, think about John and Monica
and the lessons they used to teach.

A nd now we must thank God for everything.
N o fighting, no selfishness, just be nice.
D ear Lord, thank you for everything.

M ary, Jesus and God we pray to you.
O h wonderful people for giving us some special gifts.
N ow we promise to take care and respect others around.
I n this big and dangerous world we must learn to be kind.
C are and forgive others.
A good person is always ready to forgive.

**Libby Whittingham (10)**
SS John & Monica Primary School, Moseley

## The Bright Yellow Car

It dressed up in its lovely yellow cloak,
ready to go rolling down the road.
It started to make unusual noises.
It was bleeding out oil.
It was smoking.
Its temperature raised really high.
It was flaming hot . . .
30 minutes later it died of exhaustion.
RIP.

**Jazmin Copeland (10)**
**SS John & Monica Primary School, Moseley**

## All About My Friend Georgia-Mae!

G reat at all subjects she is.
E xcited for everything, I don't know why.
O rganised she can be.
R eliable she is.
G reat and brainy, really talented.
'I don't want to go to another school,' she says.
A friend I can trust.

M ad and wild.
A mazing and wild, even wacky.
E nthusiastic in all her lessons.

    That's my friend Georgia-Mae.

**Sophie Stevens (10)**
SS John & Monica Primary School, Moseley

## Powerful Pets

Dogs, fluffy, cute and a shining light,
but at night black fur and red eyes so bright.

Fish, gold, glittery and love to swim,
at night silver, dull and has a black fin.

Cats, shiny and has lots of colours,
at night black, not like those others.

**Katie Ludlam (9)**
**St John's CE Primary School, Dudley**

## Love

I feel your tender arms around me,
putting love into my body.
It wraps around me like a big, big scarf,
warm and soft,
nothing like the cold, cold dark.

I love you just as you are,
how I know I do.
Just remember who I am,
because I'll always remember you.

**Rebecca McHale (10)**
St John's CE Primary School, Dudley

## To My Nan

How I miss you, I really do,
I wish that I was close to you,
My heart is broken, I'm really sad,
If you come back I'll be so glad.

I'm such a state, my house is a mess,
If you can't tell I feel helpless,
I sit in bed wishing you were here,
Taking over me now is my fear.

I jump out of bed and get to my feet,
The house is quiet, my family's asleep.
I look out the window then see a windmill,
Nan, I love you and always will.

**Megan Pritchard (11)**
St John's CE Primary School, Dudley

## A Fright In The Night

Paralysed in fright,
Through the long dark night,
I walked down the creaky stairs,
For one of my donkey dares.
I peeped round the corner of the door,
As I saw the big dark shadow on the floor,
I saw these wide, gleaming, yellow eyes,
As my fear suddenly dies,
I turned the light on slowly
And there was my little dog Joey.

**Georgie Roper (11)**
St John's CE Primary School, Dudley

## Friendship

My best friend giggles with glee,
When I'm sad she tickles me.
If she's poorly I take some flowers,
When she's better we play for hours.

Bullies, bullies, what can I say,
They're mean to you every day.
If my friend gets bullied I'll help her out,
*That's what friends are all about!*

**Georgina Kovacs (10)**
St John's CE Primary School, Dudley

## A Fright In The Night

As I walked in the dark night
I was paralysed with fear
I saw a shadow walking in the trees
I went up to it and saw a zombie
The zombie saw me
It grabbed me from my arm.

It took me to a house
And put me on a machine
After *ooowww!*
I was a zombie
Now waiting for the next culprit
To walk into our wrath.

**Priyesh Patel (11)**
St John's CE Primary School, Dudley

## Football Crazy

The whistle blows, off we go
What will the score be? We do not know
Whoopsie, I tripped over my lace
Who will win at the end of the race?
Me, me, me, just wait and see
To see our hearts full of glee.

**Sophie Williams (11)**
**St John's CE Primary School, Dudley**

## Crazy Animals

First I saw a dog
Sleeping like a log.
Then I saw a cat
Wearing my hat.

After that I saw another dog
Eating like a fat hog.
Then I saw a pig
Wearing an Elvis Presley wig.

Then I saw the same cat
*Hey he's now eating my hat!*
Last of all I saw a giraffe
Waiting in a café . . .

**Michael Sayers (11)**
St John's CE Primary School, Dudley

## My Best Friend

My best friend cares for me,
We have a laugh giggling with glee.
Never mind what people say,
Because we've helped each other by the end of the day.

When I'm poorly she helps me out,
She runs to me when I give her a shout.
I do that too, every day,
That's what friends do I say.

Writing this poem is really cool,
It helps children rhyme at school.
This poem is really good because
My friend helped me.

**Rachel Campion (11)**
St John's CE Primary School, Dudley

# The Football Match

I run on the pitch,
But I fall down a ditch.
All I think is this day is not going my way.
But God will help me if I pray,
But all of a sudden I can see the goal,
The fear starts to run through my soul.
I kick the ball as hard as I can,
I now think I'm the man.
They lift me up and shout with joy,
The ball is now my lethal toy.

**Pippa Humphrey (10)**
St John's CE Primary School, Dudley

## Africa

An African sunset starting the night,
As the lions end their vicious fight.
They walk home under the glowing moon,
The shining stars will be out soon.

The baby zebras are prancing around,
As elephants' slurping is one of the sounds.
The eating giraffes with their elegant neck,
As a group of ostrich peck, peck, peck.

The African flowers starting to awake,
So visit the lions for Pete's sake.

An African sunset starting the night,
As the lions end the vicious fight.
They walk home under the glowing moon,
The day will be starting soon,
For another day in Africa.

**Georgette Rudge (10)**
St John's CE Primary School, Dudley

## Something Mysterious

It was there stood in front of me,
Clear for everyone to see,
Its eyes as dark as night,
It roared giving me a fright.

It dragged me into the deep, dark wood
And it was wearing a big black hood.
It had teeth as long as pencils,
Do you know what? It collects stencils.

Did it live here on Earth
Or was it from a planet called Zenerth?
I wonder why it was here?
Did it come from my friend's ear?

**Alexandra Robinson (9)**
St John's CE Primary School, Dudley

## Cars

Zoom goes the car going very far,
Down the country lane going faster than a plane.
Engines roaring up and down,
Cars racing all year round.
Tyres burning, wheels turning.
As they race to the line,
Everyone shouts, 'Here comes mine.'

**Mitchell McCarthy (9)**
St John's CE Primary School, Dudley

## Holidays

We are going on holiday, hooray!
We need to pack straightaway.
Time to get some clothes
And have a little doze.

Yay! We are on holiday,
We flew all the way.
Put on your sunscreen,
Let's eat some ice cream.

We are back, *nooo!*
I really wanted to go.
But we can go again next year,
My mum and dad can drink some beer.

**Steph Robertson (8)**
St John's CE Primary School, Dudley

## Animals

Dogs growl,
Cats purr,
Wolves howl,
Rabbits are covered in fur,
Tigers roar,
Birds are fragile,
Leopards can always eat more,
Cheetahs can run a mile,
Elephants have long trunks,
Hippos swim in lakes,
Above the ground live chipmunks,
A nest an otter makes.

**Abigail Fear (10)**
St John's CE Primary School, Dudley

## Pirates

Pirates always make you walk the plank,
they never give you a last chance.
Pirates have a sharp sword,
they always are a bit bored.

Pirates are very fierce,
if they see you you'll get pierced.
Pirate ships are made of wood,
but watch out for sharks or you will be blood.

**Matthew Sayers (8)**
St John's CE Primary School, Dudley

## Football Match

The football match is cool
The football match rules
The crowd goes wild
When they see Kyle
When the match starts
The crowd sits down
Kyle goes up the line
And he scores a goal
What a cracker!

**Luke Stanford (9)**
St John's CE Primary School, Dudley

## My Magic Land

My magic land is where the ocean roars,
My magic land is where the waterfall pours,
My magic land is where animals dance,
My magic land is where the reindeer prance,
My magic land is where the moon glows,
My magic land is where the river flows,
My magic land will always be a secret
Just for me.

**Georgie Evans (8)**
St John's CE Primary School, Dudley

## Love

Love tastes like a sweet smell of chocolate.
Love feels like you're flying in the blue sky.
Love smells like you have a sweet smell of perfume.
Love sounds like a bird in the sky.
Love is like a bright colour.
Love reminds me of when I was born.

**Mutsa Ashley Nyamhunga (7)**
Tividale Community Primary School, Tividale

# Love

Love tastes like yummy chocolate.
Love feels like a soft, fluffy pillow.
Love smells like the sweet fragrance of a rose.
Love sounds like 'Happy Christmas'.
Love is the Pink Panther.

**Nicole Majcherczyk (7)**
**Tividale Community Primary School, Tividale**

## Hate

Hate feels like a lion roaring.
Hate smells of burning fire.
Hate sounds like people screaming.
Hate tastes of red chilli.

**Zak Tyler (7)**
**Tividale Community Primary School, Tividale**

# Hate

Hate feels like a tiger roaring at you,
Hate smells like a burning tower,
Hate tastes like a sour lemon,
Hate sounds like a wolf howling at the moon,
Its colour is as red as two burning fires,
It reminds me of a country at war with a different country.

**Gurvinder Singh (8)**
**Tividale Community Primary School, Tividale**

## Happiness

Happiness goes 'Aha, aha,' like a little kid,
Happiness tastes like a juicy sweet,
Happiness feels like your body is moving because you are
                              jumping up and down like a rabbit,
Happiness smells like cheese and tomato pizza,
Happiness makes your cheeks glow red,
Happiness reminds me of when my dad gave me sweets.

**Ekam Sandhu (8)**
Tividale Community Primary School, Tividale

## Sadness

Sadness tastes like nasty, horrible worms.
Sadness is wet and soggy.
It smells like horrible peas.
It is blue like tears and rivers.
It reminds me of someone who has died.
It sounds like someone crying.

**Courtney Bowen (7)**
Tividale Community Primary School, Tividale

## Sadness

Sadness feels like crying.
Sadness tastes like tears.
Sadness sounds like *argh!*
Sadness is the colour blue.
Sadness reminds me of forgiveness.

**Hansjit Heer (8)**
**Tividale Community Primary School, Tividale**

# Emotions

Sadness is like teardrops falling,
People dying, you're in mourning.
It feels so sad when you're there,
Emotions follow you everywhere.

Happiness is like a really fun chore,
Children laughing, it isn't a bore.
It feels so wonderful when you're there,
Emotions follow you everywhere.

Anger is like burning wood,
Red-hot rock cakes, it's not at all good.
It feels so bad when you're there,
Emotions follow you everywhere.

Emotions are not all bad,
Sometimes you're happy, sometimes you're sad.
It feels so different when you're there,
Emotions follow you everywhere.

**Pavandeep Uppal (9) & Helaina Padda (10)**
Tividale Community Primary School, Tividale

## Hallowe'en!

Haunted, spooky, scary house,
One knock at the door, for trick or treat,
Then I hear a music beat,
Someone's playing for Hallowe'en.

Haunted, spooky, scary house,
I hear an echo, a witch casting spells,
Then I see a bat flying in the sky.

Haunted, spooky, scary house,
I go inside and see a witch really casting spells,
Then I see a spider up in the roof, making webs.

Haunted, spooky, scary house,
I shouldn't have gone there for trick or treat
The witch put me in a bowl
And ate me for dinner of course!

**Smea Khan (10)**
**Tividale Community Primary School, Tividale**

# Happiness

It feels like a glow through your body,
It feels like a soft fluffy piece of cotton wool,
It is a beautiful feeling, nice and spotty.

It tastes like a nice frosted cake,
Lovely and delicious, it's nice and soothing,
It lands on you like a beautiful snowflake.

It smells like a nice piece of sweet candy,
When you have happiness, it never ends,
When you have happiness, it never goes wrong and it never bends.

It looks like a soothing sea,
You should really see it, try and have fun,
It looks so pretty, it's as powerful as the sun.

It sounds like the sea clashing and lapping,
It sounds so beautiful and gentle,
It sounds like nice holiday-type music.

It reminds me of when I get the TV all to myself,
Watch my favourite show all day,
Or when I was in the nursery doing all sorts of things,
Not having to care about anything.

**Priya Shrivastav (10)**
Tividale Community Primary School, Tividale

## Sadness And Tears

Sadness sounds like silence,
Because they are too sad to speak.
The colour of it is blue,
Like tears within the week.

It feels wet, cold and damp,
Like being in a dark, dreary cave.
It tastes dry and plain,
Not like a sweet chocolate bar crave.

It looks like a thunderstorm,
Or a dark and damp old room.
It smells like salty seawater,
Or tears in the gloom.

So tiring tears or hurt of the heart,
Are what this feels like inside.
So if you are sad or lonely, don't hide,
Just make a happiness chart.

**Demi Marriner (9)**
**Tividale Community Primary School, Tividale**

## Happiness

It looks like a shiny, shimmering sun,
a dancing fairy, as dainty as can be.

It feels like a soft cuddly cloud,
a fat teddy bear.

It sounds like birds, singing birds,
children playing on the beach.

It tastes like a big chocolate cake,
a handful of sweets.

It smells like a sea open wide,
a chocolate cake being baked.

It reminds me of children playing on the beach.

**Emma Stephenson (10)**
**Tividale Community Primary School, Tividale**

## Hate

Hate is a big bellowing bully who won't go away.
He looks like a geeky boy with pimples and a really big bum.
He smells like sour old milk that's out of date.
If Hate were a smell he would smell like someone's old gym socks.

If Hate were a taste, he would taste sour and spicy,
so bad you'd vomit with one taste.
If Hate were a sound, he would sound like a dragon
roaring and breathing out fire.

If you could feel Hate, he would feel rough and prickly,
like when you put your hand into a swarm of bees.
But if you could see Hate, he would look like a volcano
that won't stop erupting. *Bang!*

**Jhanee Wilkins (10)**
Tividale Community Primary School, Tividale

# Happiness

She is a girlie girl,
Dressed in pretty pink,
She prances around all the sad people,
And gives them a little wink.

When she gives you a wink,
She sure makes you smile,
But use it when you can,
It only lasts a while.

She makes you feel soft,
Like a little teddy bear,
She makes you feel nice,
But shout, don't you dare!

Happiness is like the sun,
Big, yellow and bright,
Happiness won't make you fear,
She won't give you a fright.

Happiness reminds me of my birthday,
When everybody comes around,
Happiness reminds me of my birthday,
When no one wears a frown.

Happiness smells of perfume,
She smells of flowers too,
If I find you frowning,
I'll help you get through.

**Simrun Bains (10)**
**Tividale Community Primary School, Tividale**

## Anger

Anger tastes like burning fire,
Anger feels like a bee stinging someone,
Anger smells like a donkey,
Anger sounds like an ugly monster,
Anger's colours are red and black,
Anger reminds me of my teddy.

**Luqman Ahmed (7)**
**Tividale Community Primary School, Tividale**

# Love

Love is like a soft snowball and Cupid's angel,
She smells like fresh flowers,
She tastes like melted chocolate,
She looks like a ribbon in a heart,
She sounds like lovely music,
She feels like joy in your heart,
She reminds me of lovely fresh roses.

**Satnam Kaur (9)**
**Tividale Community Primary School, Tividale**

## Anger

Anger is burning flames, hot -
He smells like hot pepper burning.
He tastes like bitter lemon on my mouth.
He feels like trees burning.
He sounds like noise getting closer and closer.
Anger looks like a furious face.
He reminds me of a bad birthday.

**Idris Hussain (9)**
Tividale Community Primary School, Tividale

## Anger

Anger is like burning trees on the ground
and spicy food burning in your mouth.

She smells like cracking branches.

She sounds like angry thunder in the dark
and lightning flashes in the sky.

She tastes like an angry apple and bitter lemons
in your mouth.

Anger looks like fighting children,
loudly shouting at each other.

She feels like burning hands and red faces
in the moonlight.

She reminds me of black burning fields.

**Olivia Sodhi (10)**
**Tividale Community Primary School, Tividale**

# Happiness

Happiness is a bright blue sky and a colourful rainbow.
He smells like beautiful roses.
He tastes like sweet oranges in your mouth.
He sounds like the birds singing; see the children playing loudly.
Happiness looks like a great thing.
He feels like a fun book of funny pictures.
He reminds me of when it was my birthday and my party.
Never let happiness go away.

**Christopher Lal (10)**
Tividale Community Primary School, Tividale

## Love

Love is roses waving in the breeze.
She smells like sweet strawberries on a plate.
Love reminds me of my nan when she was alive.

**Nick Evans (10)**
Tividale Community Primary School, Tividale

## Love

Love is a red rose from Heaven,
She smells like lovely lemons drifting by,
She tastes like pears with dreams,
She sounds like tweeting birds singing to each other,
Love looks like eyes looking into other eyes,
She feels like stroking birds with your hand,
She reminds me of when I was born.

**Nathan Biran (10)**
Tividale Community Primary School, Tividale

## Happiness

Happiness is flowers floating across the blue sky,
It smells like red tomatoes growing up from the ground,
It sounds like brand new books,
Happiness looks like white clouds making a flower,
It feels like the bright moon in the sky,
It reminds me of going on holiday on a ferry.

**Dhiren Patel (9)**
**Tividale Community Primary School, Tividale**

## Love, Love, Love

Love is like jumping dolphins playing in the sea.
She smells like sweet strawberries in a dish with ice cream.
She tastes like melted chocolate dripping from a spoon.
She feels like chocolate cooking in a saucepan.
Love looks like people playing happily in the park
She feels like a puppy on my bed.
She reminds me of my nan when she buys me presents.

**Rebecca Shepherd (9)**
**Tividale Community Primary School, Tividale**

## Love

Love is like the sea's waves splashing onto the shore.
She smells like food, hot and spicy.
She tastes like air, soft and cool.
She sounds like soft sweet music playing away.
She looks like the birds flying away.
She feels like softness when sleeping on a bed.
She reminds me of when I was born.

**Kiranpreet Hayer (10)**
**Tividale Community Primary School, Tividale**

## Anger

Anger is like fumes coming out of an exhaust pipe,
He smells like burning wood,
He tastes bitter like a lemon,
He sounds like thunder and lightning on a rainy day,
Anger looks like a lion tearing open a sheep when he is furious,
He feels spiky like a hedgehog,
He reminds me of a ghostly wind in the trees.

**Hussnain Anwar (10)**
Tividale Community Primary School, Tividale

## Love

Love is a red rose from Heaven,
She smells like sweet lemons drifting by,
She tastes like pears with ice cream,
She sounds like a drum banging loudly,
Love looks like a butterfly fluttering slowly,
She feels like sugar melting slowly,
She reminds me of my birthday and having lots of fun.

**Abbey Glancey (9)**
Tividale Community Primary School, Tividale

## Sadness

Sadness is like salty water in a jug.
She smells like cinnamon in a jar.
She tastes like sour lemons.
She sounds like a harp playing a low tune.
Sadness looks like a broken heart.
She feels like a rough jumper.
She reminds me of my grandad.

**Ben Millward (10)**
Tividale Community Primary School, Tividale

# Love

Love is like jumping dolphins in the sea.
He smells like a bunch of flowers.
He tastes like sweet strawberries.
He sounds like sweet music.
He looks like big love hearts floating in the sky.
He reminds me of the times I spent go-kart racing.

**Kieran Bowen (9)**
**Tividale Community Primary School, Tividale**

## Feelings

Happy times are nice and soft like a bed or a cushion.
When the sweet birds sing in the bright light.
Happy times smell just like sweet food cooking in the hot,
burning frying pan.
When the food is ready we hear children and adults
enjoying themselves.
The food tastes like sweet apples shining on a branch in the
beautiful bright sky.

Sadness is like starving children and people dying.

Anger feels like a volcano exploding and also an earthquake.

**Jaspreet Kaur Rayat (7)**
Tividale Community Primary School, Tividale

## Emotions

Anger feels like someone is shooting at you.
Happiness makes you gleeful.
Anger feels like someone slapping you.
Happiness feels like you are eating a chocolate cake.
Anger feels like someone bullying you.
Happiness feels like you are going on holiday.

**Gurpreet Kaur (7)**
Tividale Community Primary School, Tividale

# Love

Love is a sign of angels,
It smells like roses in the air,
It tastes like melted chocolate flowing in the sky,
It sounds like twinkling music,
Love looks like red fluffy cushions,
It feels like a heart beating,
It reminds me of real hearts in the air.

**Jordan Basra**
**Tividale Community Primary School, Tividale**

## Anger

Anger is like a very smoky fire that burns everything on top of it.
He smells like completely pitch-black smoke.
He tastes like a dirty, ripped, woolly rug.
He sounds like very loud thunder banging against my window
                                                                                        in the dark.
Anger looks like a very cold ice cube.
He feels like very hot chilli on your tongue.
He reminds me of when I lost my special toy car.

**Samvir Sandhu (9)**
Tividale Community Primary School, Tividale

# Emotions

*Upset*
Upset feels like starving children in Africa.
Upset smells like tears dropping on your nose.
Upset looks like people stamping on you.
Upset tastes like sour lemons.
Upset sounds like people crying on comfy cushions.

*Happiness*
Happiness feels like people drinking steaming hot chocolate.
Happiness smells like fresh cake in the bakery.
Happiness looks like children playing in big gardens.
Happiness tastes like double runny ice cream.
Happiness sounds like adults having a laugh.

**Prabhjeet Gill (8)**
Tividale Community Primary School, Tividale

# When I Feel . . .

*Jolly*
Jolly feels like you are special.
Jolly looks like cheerful children giggling.
Jolly tastes like wibbly wobbly jelly.
Jolly smells like creamy custard.
Jolly sounds like a world of music.

*Upset*
Upset feels like people treading and stamping on you.
Upset tastes like burning lava from a volcano.
Upset smells like burning wood.
Upset looks like starving children everywhere.
Upset sounds like people crying and crying.

**Sharonjit Kaur Dhinsa (8)**
Tividale Community Primary School, Tividale

# Happiness And Sadness

*Happiness*
Happiness smells like lovely chocolate milkshake.
Happiness sounds like I've got lots of money.
Happiness looks like the shiny blue sea.
Happiness feels like everybody's wearing a smile.
Happiness looks like the golden class and everything golden.

*Sadness*
Sadness feels like everybody is sad.
Sadness sounds like everybody's not playing and they're not happy.
Sadness tastes like no one is smiling.
Sadness feels like some people are fighting.

**Zaina Yousaf (8)**
**Tividale Community Primary School, Tividale**

# Emotions

Happiness feels like you're the happiest person in the world.
Happiness smells like a big room of joyful people.

Anger feels like you're a volcano erupting with embers shooting out.
Anger smells like a burning volcano.
Anger feels like you're going to blow up.

Happiness feels you're a joyful person.
Happiness smells like fresh flowers.
Happiness feels like you're cuddling a huge cushion.

Anger feels like a room of fury.
Anger feels like you want to punch and kick someone.
Anger smells like burning ash.

**Parvathan Singh Biran (7)**
Tividale Community Primary School, Tividale

## Anger And Happiness

Happiness sounds like fresh flowers in the morning.
Happiness feels like a big block of joy.

Anger sounds like a big volcano going to explode.
Anger looks like a shed on fire.

Happiness smells like a creamy hot cappuccino.

Sadness looks like flames rising.

Happiness is like a golden river streaming along to the sunset.

Sadness sounds like a river that has sharks.

**Navina Sahota (8)**
Tividale Community Primary School, Tividale

## Jolly Poems And Sad Poems

Happy feels jolly in a park with flowers in the air.
Happy is hearing a butterfly flying in the air.
Happy is seeing a rabbit walking across a shop.
Happiness is going to the café with a big slice of cake.

Cross is seeing the sky going as red as a rose.
Cross is hitting a wall and walking away.
Cross is a bulb growing into a flower.

**Rajdeep Kaur Sahota (8)**
**Tividale Community Primary School, Tividale**

# Emotions

Excitement feels like playing in a garden of laughter.
Excitement smells like a picnic with yummy chocolates.
Excitement looks like a moonlit night.
Excitement, you could say it was a beautiful crystal.

Sadness smells like fire.
Sadness looks like bullying.
Sadness feels like a brick crashing to the ground.
Sadness sounds like a baby crying.
Sadness is bad like something burning.

Anger smells like a burning fire.
Anger looks like a monster.
Anger feels like a hundred people shouting.
Anger sounds like roaring.
Anger is like nasty people.

**Nikki Grewal (7)**
Tividale Community Primary School, Tividale

## Happy And Anger

Happy feels like a cuddly cushion.
Happy tastes like melted milk - nice cold ice cream.
Happy looks like when you are happy.
Happy smells like you're looking at the sunrise.

Anger looks like burning hot, dark coal.
Anger tastes like people are hot and the sun is burning you.
Anger feels like burning lava on your hand.
Anger smells of people burning.

**Jaghuir Singh (7)**
Tividale Community Primary School, Tividale

## My Poem About Feelings

Happiness feels like bubbly drinking chocolate.
Happiness feels like a hot bath.
Happiness feels like the children playing in the park.
Happiness feels like the breeze blowing towards you.
Happiness feels like listening to music.

**Parris Rowley (7)**
Tividale Community Primary School, Tividale

# Emotions

Anger feels like burning hot embers.
Anger tastes like a volcano just going to erupt.
Anger smells like burning wood.

Happiness feels soft and comfortable like a soft bed.
Happiness tastes like soft sticky toffee.

Sadness feels like a war and people bite.
Sadness tastes like you are being hit.

**Jamie Fulwell (7)**
**Tividale Community Primary School, Tividale**

## Feelings

Excitement feels like a big orange teddy bear
and you're asleep on it all day.

Anger feels like a monster has taken over your body.

Excitement looks like the land of your dreams.

**Gian Randhawa (8)**
**Tividale Community Primary School, Tividale**

## Happiness And Anger

Happiness looks like a golden chest of shiny gold.
Happiness feels like a giant fluffy bed.
Happiness smells like fresh cakes in the oven.
Happiness tastes like bubbly chocolate, freshly made.
Happiness sounds like gold coins falling from the sky.

Anger looks like a giant volcano erupting.
Anger feels like you want to scream.
Anger smells like embers of a burning fire.
Anger tastes like burning hot sweets.
Anger sounds like fire getting bigger in a wooden tree.

**Katie Maria Ubhi (7)**
**Tividale Community Primary School, Tividale**

## Fear

Fear, fear sounds like a screech
That is going round your dizzy head.

It looks like a jail that is dark and scary,
And the gates are closed and there's nowhere to get out,
All the horrible creatures wriggling on my bed.

It smells like fear and pain coming your way,
So be very quick to move,
And you better listen to what I say.

It feels like snails swirling and shaking,
When I don't understand what's happening,
While I'm baking.

It tastes of sickness coming up your throat,
It reminds me of a day when I fell sick.

**Kiran Sandhu (10)**
**Tividale Community Primary School, Tividale**

## Silence

Silence is the opposite to noise,
It's peaceful,
It's more silent than snow,
It feels like soft smooth snow,
It feels as though no one's there,
It reminds you of the days full of joy,
It tastes savoury,
It smells like bread that has just been baked,
It sounds like a quiet day,
Looks like nothing's there.

**Kiranjit Kaur Rai (9)**
Tividale Community Primary School, Tividale

# Silence Poem

He looks very pale,
Runny like ale,
Speechless as a serpent,
Like a flower without its scent.

He looks as if he has been whitewashed,
But now no one can find him,
No soul can find him,
Because he is lost.

He sounds so quiet, it's deafening,
Like the birds in the sky have scattered and left him,
Like his eyes poke you in the back and you feel him staring.

Like a candle that doesn't give any light,
Like fire that doesn't provide heat,
He scares me,
Just like the darkness of the night.

**Priya Rai (10)**
Tividale Community Primary School, Tividale

## Anger

He has a rough, fat belly and red tomato cheeks,
He sounds like a volcano as he walks round to school
With his fat, hairy legs,
He smells like burning wood, like chilli peppers burning.

He feels like rough skin that has come off a rotten apple,
He looks like a red chilli pepper.

He sounds like a volcano ready to break out,
He feels like a rough orange.

**Olivia Hall (10)**
Tividale Community Primary School, Tividale

## Fuzzy Fun

If fun were a colour, it would be
Orange and yellow balloons
floating in the air.

If fun were a smell,
it would smell like
perfume, oranges and lemons.

If fun were a look,
it would look like
blue and pink clouds waving.

Fun reminds me of me
playing in the fabulous
fun sun!

*Fuzzy, fab, fun!*

**Sanna Mahmood (9)**
Tividale Community Primary School, Tividale

## Fear

Fear is like a snake that's waiting for a victim for its own feast.
It smells like blood on a dead body.
It tastes like a bitter lemon.
It sounds like burning fumes in a wild forest.
It looks like the Devil killing for amusement.
It feels like a snake that moves so slowly it feels as though it's
                                                on your spine.
It reminds me of a snake that caught me on my leg.

**Takudzwa Mudere (10)**
Tividale Community Primary School, Tividale

## Happiness And Anger

Happiness feels like the wind blowing slowly through your hair.
Happiness sounds like children playing joyfully.
Happiness tastes like laughing potion.
Happiness smells like fresh, beautiful roses.

Anger feels like burning lava.
Anger sounds like a massive volcano has exploded.
Anger tastes like burning hot fire from a volcano.
Anger smells like burning toast.
Anger looks like horrible flames burning brightly.

**Natasha Thompson (8)**
Tividale Community Primary School, Tividale

# Emotions

Anger feels like you've been shot by a gun.
Anger sounds like a child screaming for help.
Anger tastes like bright red blood.
Anger smells like dead rats.
Anger looks like war.

Happiness feels like a bluebird's feathers falling from the sky.
Happiness feels like birds tweeting in the sky.
Happiness tastes like creamy toffee.

**Jerome Sylvester (8)**
**Tividale Community Primary School, Tividale**

## Feelings And Emotions

Happiness feels like you're eating a bubbly chocolate.
Happiness smells like a fresh flower.
Happiness looks like a big smile in a forest.
Happiness tastes like a big jelly in a house.
Happiness sounds like a gang of birds singing.

Sadness feels like a baby crying.
Sadness sounds like an aeroplane exploding.
Sadness looks like a train crashing.
Sadness tastes like a volcano erupting.
Sadness smells like a house exploding.

**Callum Welborn (8)**
Tividale Community Primary School, Tividale

## Happiness

Happiness makes you smile,
Happiness makes you feel joyful,
Happiness doesn't make you cry,
Happiness makes you smile all the time.

**Ranjna Dewit (8)**
Tividale Community Primary School, Tividale

## Anger

Anger is a sudden roar of hate and revenge,
A blast of fire never-ending in your head,
But if anger were a taste, it would taste of hot chilli and sour soup.

The pungent smell of anger leaks everywhere and you can't escape,
The look of this horrible emotion is like a lion ripping off someone's
                                                                                     skin by your feet.

The sound of this emotion is like a thunderous boom right in your ear,
And the feeling of icy cold air as cold as liquid nitrogen.

**Makaita Kanyuchi (10)**
**Tividale Community Primary School, Tividale**

## Anger

Anger is like a grumpy grandad sitting in his old and tatty chair.
He sits there smelling like mouldy, milk, he's always grumpy
and smelly.
It always feels like a volcano vibrating in your stomach.
Your face turns red and you start to sweat and you get very angry
and your breath starts to smell like sour soup so you start to feel
angry, walk away and tell a teacher, because it's not nice to feel
angry; just listen to what I say and never feel angry.
Thank you.

**Macauley Scott (9)**
**Tividale Community Primary School, Tividale**

## Laughter

It feels like fluffy flowers,
It looks like a fluffy bunny,
It sounds like a tickly feeling in my tummy,
It tastes like a creamy cake,
It smells like a joyful day.

It reminds me of you!

**Sukhjit Johal (9)**
**Tividale Community Primary School, Tividale**

## Silence

Stunning silence,
    Stopping the words;
        No sound,
            No hooting birds.

Clear silence,
    Stops the way
        Of talking, yap, yap.
            Keeps it at bay.

Stopping silence,
    Shutting up;
        Ring around your neck,
            Not even a cracking cup.

Shutting silence,
    No slamming door;
        No talking,
            Not anymore.

**Nuna Vondee Gohoho (10)**
Tividale Community Primary School, Tividale

## Laughter

Everyone likes her, as you can see,
everyone looks after her and keeps her company.
We can feel her and she feels like a feather,
she has a different name, but we all call her Heather.

If I could bottle laughter, it would surely look like a mouth
smiling at me, and this is how much I took:

I took lots and lots, my bottle is almost full
and now I've got to put it all into a cup.

**Ishmael Huxtable-Rowe (10)**
Tividale Community Primary School, Tividale

## Laughter

It looks like a shimmering shiny sun,
It sounds like children laughing and having fun,
It tastes like a sweet biscuit crumb,
It reminds me of a hot sunny sun,
It feels like a soft smooth sponge.

**Navdeep Kaur Heer (10)**
Tividale Community Primary School, Tividale

## The Sadness Of Life

Sadness sounds like a dead dog wailing its last seconds of life away,
It smells like a child crying away pain from a deadly disease,
It looks like a family pet ebbing away at the pain of death.

Sadness feels lumpy and firm but not too strong,
It reminds me of awful things from the past,
But most of all, sadness reminds us of our worst nightmares.

**Niall Hughes (9)**
**Tividale Community Primary School, Tividale**

# Hate

He is big and blazing,
He has got no friends at all,
He is hurtfully lonely and separate from us,
He never catches the bus
With the rest of us.

He sits in the corner all alone,
I often wonder if he is a clone,
He sits and moans all alone,
Has he got a home?
I don't know if he is all alone.

The clashing and the clattering,
The burning, the thudding,
The loneliness, is he alone?
All alone?

**Laura Cowley (9)**
**Tividale Community Primary School, Tividale**

# Fun

It feels slimy and soft like a pillow.
It looks like a fluffy cake with red and blue icing.
It looks like a furry, funny fairy whizzing everywhere,
that is very, very happy.
The furry, funny fairy goes and makes everyone happy,
she smells like a lavender flower and she will turn into any colour
she can think of.
She goes *swish, swash* and *twinkle* with her wand
turning sadness into joy.
She reminds me of the time I went to Canada, playing with
my little brother all day.

**Bhavin Patel (10)**
Tividale Community Primary School, Tividale

# Happiness

Happiness tastes sweet as a pineapple,
Happiness feels as smooth as a sheep's skin,
Happiness' colour is as shiny as a brown face,
Happiness sounds as soft as a beautiful sunny day,
Happiness reminds me of when I was on the swings,
Happiness smells as nice as a beautiful tree.

**Sonia Virk (8)**
**Tividale Community Primary School, Tividale**

## A Witch . . .

My name is Beth
And I am not embarrassed to say
That I am a witch
Don't be afraid of me
Because I don't cast spells
Or hex.
I wear a cape
But not a pointy hat
I know you might be scared
But play with me
Don't run away from me
My teacher says that witches aren't real
So is he saying I'm not real?
Is he saying that I'm invisible?
Don't worry, I don't fly on a broom
'Cause I am a more technological witch
Because I fly on a vacuum.

**Bethany Jones (11)**
Woodgate Primary School, Birmingham

## Clouds

Clouds are candyfloss floating in the air,
They are lovely shapes flying above us,
Clouds are a piece of fluff lying in the sky.
Clouds are wonderful things.

**Jamie Ashmore (11)**
Woodgate Primary School, Birmingham

## Horses And Ponies - Haiku

Horses are the best
You can make them jump and trot
Ponies are so cute.

**Rosie Jones (11)**
Woodgate Primary School, Birmingham

## Snow - Haiku

The wind blows the snow
Snow is great to get payback
Snow makes it get cold.

**Charlotte Whatmore (10)**
Woodgate Primary School, Birmingham

## Hailstones - Haiku

It has a cold touch
*Clip, clap, clop* on your ceiling
Hurts when it comes down.

**Daniel Hancock (10)**
Woodgate Primary School, Birmingham

## Earth - Haiku

Is it rotating?
I can feel it every day.
Can you feel it too?

**Amy Le (10)**
Woodgate Primary School, Birmingham

## My Garden

My garden is not big, but it's not too small,
There's room for us all,
There's room for a swing and a slide,
Plenty of space to have a race.
The grass is green, the trees are tall
Dandelions are yellow, daisies are white
Put them together so they become bright.

**Courtney Ward (8) & Kodey Williams (10)**
Woodgate Primary School, Birmingham

## England

E xcellent football players
N ew shiny boots
G errard is a star
L inesman flagging for offside
A mazing football stars
N ever lose, always win
D ream of winning the World Cup.

**Christopher Reeves (11)**
Woodgate Primary School, Birmingham

## Mice

I think mice
are rather nice.
They live in a house
with no one else.
There is a mouse
down the street
and there is a cat
waiting for a feast.
The mouse gets eaten
by the cat.
Now he is big and fat!

**Gary Howard (10)**
**Woodgate Primary School, Birmingham**

## Blues - Haiku

They really are best.
They play in a stadium.
Blues are excellent.

**Joshua Saunders (10)**
Woodgate Primary School, Birmingham

## Nasty Rhyme

One wicked witch
Two terrible teachers
Three fearsome fangs
Four frightening flying frogs
Five flies flying
Six snakes slithering
Seven scorpions scurrying
Eight eggs in an empty box
Nine nasty nits
Ten terrifying tarantulas.

**Calam Oakley (11)**
**Woodgate Primary School, Birmingham**

## The Moon

The moon is a football
It is like a pancake
Or a big fat cheese
The moon lives up in the sky
It never goes down
It is a silver coin.

**Amie Atkinson (10)**
Woodgate Primary School, Birmingham

## Snowman

S nowy day outside
N ew crispy flakes
O ften feels cold
W iggly outside
M ake snowman
A round in winter season
N ice cold snow.

**Brendan Snow (11)**
**Woodgate Primary School, Birmingham**

# Winter

W ater is cold,
I t will turn into ice,
N ever go outside,
T ears will freeze,
E ars of children are so red,
R eal living creatures will die instead.

**Sophie Kelly (10)**
Woodgate Primary School, Birmingham

## Animals

Fluffy kittens play with wool
Cute puppies chew the door
Baby birds creep to Mom
Goldfish *plop, plop* around the bowl
Lizzy lizards catching flies
Silly bear's lost his fish
Now they're all in bed fast asleep, *zzzz*.

**Nicole Goff (11)**
**Woodgate Primary School, Birmingham**

## The Big Blue Box

The big blue box
appears in time
the owner
battles crime
it's disguised
in a fashioned theme
it has on the top
a light that beams
it's had its times
throughout the world.

**Christopher Fisher (11)**
**Woodgate Primary School, Birmingham**

## My Team

A rsenal is the best
R osicky runs around
S uper soccer
E verton lose to Arsenal
N o one beats Arsenal
A liens are invading Arsenal
L iving in luxury.

**Dylan Lee (11)**
**Woodgate Primary School, Birmingham**

## Aston Villa

A ston Villa is the best team
S orenson is the best goalkeeper
T rouble in the crowd
O 'Neill is the manager but a bit crazy
N ot that loud but fans are

V ictory for Villa when they win
I ncredible goal for Burso when he scores
L osers go away
L inesman waves the flag when you are offside
A nother good game next.

**Jack Bissell (11)**
**Woodgate Primary School, Birmingham**

## Blues, Blues, Blues

Blues are the best, Blues are fun,
Blues are fashionable, Blues are good,
They're gonna win the Championship.
Let's hope they're gonna win,
Then they'll be the very best,
Blues win, *yes!*

**Rebecca Allcott (10)**
Woodgate Primary School, Birmingham

## The Sun

The sun is a fireball burning so hot.
It is like a football.
It's a lion with a big mane.
The sun is a basketball
That has been put in the sky.
The sun is an orange in the sky.
The sun is a big red star.
The sun.

**Matthew Morgan (11)**
Woodgate Primary School, Birmingham

# Summer

S unny and hot
U p and up in the sky
M others sit down and rest
M elting ice cream
E ach ice cream I eat
R estful breezes.

**Jade Johnson (10)**
Woodgate Primary School, Birmingham

## Rock! - Haiku

'Lectric guitars rock,
*Pick, pick,* go the guitar strings.
Makes you feel alive.

**Lauren-Annie Lintott (11)**
**Woodgate Primary School, Birmingham**

## Lightning - Haiku

Lightning is so loud
It makes you get an earache
It is very bright.

**Amy Harrison (10)**
**Woodgate Primary School, Birmingham**

## Horses - Haiku

Horses go *clip-clop*
Horses are intelligent
They can be noisy.

**Katie Donnelly (10)**
**Woodgate Primary School, Birmingham**

## The Ocean - Haiku

Graceful but vicious
Sometimes it has such big waves
Listen to it whoosh.

**Natalie Eddington (11)**
Woodgate Primary School, Birmingham

## The Ocean - Haiku

You can swim in it
The big waves splash in the wind
The water is blue.

**Victoria Boucher (11)**
**Woodgate Primary School, Birmingham**

## Movies - Haiku

I like horror ones.
I do not like romance ones.
Movies are so great.

**Jack Strutt (11)**
Woodgate Primary School, Birmingham

# Rubbish!

Rubbish, rubbish
here and there.
Rubbish, rubbish
*everywhere!*

Rubbish, rubbish
is so messy.
Rubbish, rubbish
is not named Bessie.
Rubbish, rubbish
here and there.
Rubbish, rubbish
*everywhere!*

Rubbish, rubbish
is so smelly.
Rubbish, rubbish
could hurt your belly.
Rubbish, rubbish
here and there.
Rubbish, rubbish
*everywhere!*

Rubbish, rubbish
is lots of fun.
Rubbish, rubbish
is hated by mums.
Rubbish, rubbish
here and there.
Rubbish, rubbish
*everywhere!*

**Jessica Cammack (10)**
**Woodgate Primary School, Birmingham**

## The Moon Is A Football

The moon is a football up in the sky,
it never comes down so don't even try.
The moon is a pancake up in the air,
it's waiting for you, you'd better go now!

**Jennifer Hunt (10)**
Woodgate Primary School, Birmingham

## Young Writers Information

We hope you have enjoyed reading this book - and that you will continue to enjoy it in the coming years.

If you like reading and writing poetry drop us a line, or give us a call, and we'll send you a free information pack.

Alternatively if you would like to order further copies of this book or any of our other titles, then please give us a call or log onto our website at www.youngwriters.co.uk

**Young Writers Information**
**Remus House**
**Coltsfoot Drive**
**Peterborough**
**PE2 9JX**

**(01733) 890066**